Plant Name	**Date Planted**

Water Requirements 💧 💧💧 💧💧💧

Sunlight ☀ ☀ ⬤

☐ Seed ☐ Transplant

Date	Event

Notes

Outcome

Uses

Purchased at: _______________________________   Price: ___________

Plant Name   **Date Planted**

Water
Requirements   💧 💧💧 💧💧💧   Sunlight   ☀ ◑ ●

☐ Seed   ☐ Transplant

Date	Event

Notes

Outcome

Uses

Purchased at: ________________________________   Price: ________________

Plant Name   **Date Planted**

Water
Requirements   💧   💧💧   💧💧💧   Sunlight   ☀   ◐   ●

☐ Seed   ☐ Transplant

Date	Event

Notes

Outcome

Uses

Purchased at: _______________________________   Price: _______________

Plant Name	**Date Planted**

Water Requirements   Sunlight

☐ Seed   ☐ Transplant

Date	Event

Notes

Outcome

Uses

Purchased at: ____   Price: ________________

Plant Name

Date Planted

Water
Requirements

Sunlight

☐ Seed　　☐ Transplant

Date	Event

Notes

Outcome

Uses

Purchased at: _______________________________________　　Price: _______________________

Plant Name   **Date Planted**

Water
Requirements   Sunlight

☐ Seed   ☐ Transplant

Date	Event

Notes

Outcome

Uses

Purchased at: _______________________________________   Price: _______________

Plant Name | **Date Planted**

Water Requirements 💧 💧💧 💧💧💧

Sunlight

☐ Seed   ☐ Transplant

Date	Event

Notes

Outcome

Uses

Purchased at: _______________________________   Price: _______________________

Plant Name	**Date Planted**

Water Requirements 🌢 🌢🌢 🌢🌢🌢

Sunlight ☀ ☀ ⬤

☐ Seed   ☐ Transplant

Date	Event

Notes

Outcome

Uses

Purchased at: ________________________________   Price: ____________

Plant Name	**Date Planted**

Water Requirements 💧 💧💧 💧💧💧

Sunlight ☀ ◐ ●

☐ Seed ☐ Transplant

Date	Event

Notes

Outcome

Uses

Purchased at: ________________________ Price: ________________________

Plant Name

Date Planted

Water
Requirements

Sunlight

☐ Seed   ☐ Transplant

Date	Event

Notes

Outcome

Uses

Purchased at: _______________________   Price: _______________

Plant Name   **Date Planted**

Water
Requirements

Sunlight

☐ Seed   ☐ Transplant

Date	Event

Notes

Outcome

Uses

Purchased at: ____   Price: ____________________

Plant Name   **Date Planted**

Water
Requirements 💧   💧💧   💧💧💧   Sunlight ☀ ☀ ⬤

☐ Seed   ☐ Transplant

Date	Event

Notes

Outcome

Uses

Purchased at: _______________________________________   Price: _______________________

Plant Name **Date Planted**

Water Requirements 💧 💧💧 💧💧💧

Sunlight ☀ ☀ ●

☐ Seed ☐ Transplant

Date	Event

Notes

Outcome

Uses

Purchased at: ________________________________ Price: ________________________________

Plant Name	**Date Planted**

Water Requirements 💧 💧💧 💧💧💧   Sunlight ☀ ◑ ⬤

☐ Seed   ☐ Transplant

Date	Event

Notes

Outcome

Uses

Purchased at: _______________________________   Price: _______________

Plant Name

Date Planted

Water Requirements

Sunlight

Seed

Transplant

Date	Event

Notes

Outcome

Uses

Purchased at: ________________________

Price: ________________________

Plant Name	**Date Planted**

Water Requirements

Sunlight

☐ Seed ☐ Transplant

Date	Event

Notes

Outcome

Uses

Purchased at: ____ Price: ______________

Plant Name   **Date Planted**

Water Requirements   🌢 🌢🌢 🌢🌢🌢   Sunlight ☼ ◑ ●

☐ Seed   ☐ Transplant

Date	Event

Notes

Outcome

Uses

Purchased at: ______________________________   Price: ______________________

Plant Name	**Date Planted**

Water Requirements   💧   💧💧   💧💧💧

Sunlight   ☀   ◑   ●

☐ Seed   ☐ Transplant

Date	Event

Notes

Outcome

Uses

Purchased at: _______________________________   Price: _______________

Plant Name	**Date Planted**

Water Requirements 💧 💧💧 💧💧💧

Sunlight ☀ ◐ ●

☐ Seed   ☐ Transplant

Date	Event

Notes

Outcome

Uses

Purchased at: _______________________   Price: _______________

Plant Name Date Planted

Water Requirements Sunlight

☐ Seed ☐ Transplant

Date	Event

Notes

Outcome

Uses

Purchased at: _______________________________________ Price: _______________

Plant Name	**Date Planted**

Water Requirements 💧 💧💧 💧💧💧

Sunlight ☀ ☀ ⬤

☐ Seed ☐ Transplant

Date	Event

Notes

Outcome

Uses

Purchased at: ________________________   Price: ________________________

Plant Name   **Date Planted**

Water
Requirements

Sunlight

☐ Seed   ☐ Transplant

Date	Event

Notes

Outcome

Uses

Purchased at: _______________________________________   Price: _________________

Plant Name

Date Planted

Water Requirements

Sunlight

Seed

Transplant

Date	Event

Notes

Outcome

Uses

Purchased at: _______________________

Price: _______________________

Plant Name

Date Planted

Water
Requirements

Sunlight

☐ Seed   ☐ Transplant

Date	Event

Notes

Outcome

Uses

Purchased at: _______________________________   Price: ___________

Plant Name	Date Planted

Water Requirements

Sunlight

☐ Seed   ☐ Transplant

Date	Event

Notes

Outcome

Uses

Purchased at: _______________________   Price: _______________________

Plant Name

Date Planted

Water Requirements

Sunlight

Seed

Transplant

Date	Event

Notes

Outcome

Uses

Purchased at: ____

Price: _______________

Plant Name	**Date Planted**

Water Requirements

Sunlight

☐ Seed ☐ Transplant

Date	Event

Notes

Outcome

Uses

Purchased at: _____________________________ Price: _____________________

Plant Name   **Date Planted**

Water
Requirements   💧   💧💧   💧💧💧

Sunlight   ☀ ☀ ⬤

☐ Seed   ☐ Transplant

Date	Event

Notes

Outcome

Uses

Purchased at: _______________________________________   Price: _______________

Plant Name   **Date Planted**

Water
Requirements   🌢   🌢🌢   🌢🌢🌢   Sunlight   ☀ ☀ ●

☐ Seed   ☐ Transplant

Date	Event

Notes

Outcome

Uses

Purchased at: ___________________________   Price: ___________________

Plant Name

Date Planted

Water Requirements

Sunlight

☐ Seed   ☐ Transplant

Date	Event

Notes

Outcome

Uses

Purchased at: _______________________   Price: _______________________

Plant Name

Date Planted

Water
Requirements

Sunlight

☐ Seed   ☐ Transplant

Date	Event

Notes

Outcome

Uses

Purchased at: _______________________________   Price: _______________________________

Plant Name

Date Planted

Water Requirements

Sunlight

Seed

Transplant

Date	Event

Notes

Outcome

Uses

Purchased at: ____   Price: _______________

Plant Name	**Date Planted**

Water Requirements

Sunlight

☐ Seed   ☐ Transplant

Date	Event

Notes

Outcome

Uses

Purchased at: _______________________   Price: _______________________

Plant Name   **Date Planted**

Water
Requirements

Sunlight

☐ Seed   ☐ Transplant

Date	Event

Notes

Outcome

Uses

Purchased at: ________________________________   Price: ____________

Plant Name	**Date Planted**

Water Requirements

Sunlight

☐ Seed ☐ Transplant

Date	Event

Notes

Outcome

Uses

Purchased at: ________________________ Price: ________________________

Plant Name   **Date Planted**

Water
Requirements 💧 💧💧 💧💧💧   Sunlight ☀ ☀ ●

☐ Seed   ☐ Transplant

Date	Event

Notes

Outcome

Uses

Purchased at: ____   Price: _______________

Plant Name   **Date Planted**

Water
Requirements 💧   💧💧   💧💧💧   Sunlight ☀ ◐ ●

☐ Seed   ☐ Transplant

Date	Event

Notes

Outcome

Uses

Purchased at: ___________________________   Price: ___________________

Plant Name **Date Planted**

Water Requirements 🌢 🌢🌢 🌢🌢🌢   Sunlight ☼ ◐ ●

☐ Seed   ☐ Transplant

Date	Event

Notes

Outcome

Uses

Purchased at: _______________________________________   Price: _______________

Plant Name	**Date Planted**

Water Requirements

Sunlight

☐ Seed   ☐ Transplant

Date	Event

Notes

Outcome

Uses

Purchased at: _______________________   Price: _______________________

Plant Name   **Date Planted**

Water
Requirements   Sunlight

☐ Seed   ☐ Transplant

Date	Event

Notes

Outcome

Uses

Purchased at: ___________________________________   Price: ___________

Plant Name	**Date Planted**

Water Requirements

Sunlight

☐ Seed   ☐ Transplant

Date	Event

Notes

Outcome

Uses

Purchased at: _______________________   Price: _______________________

<table>
<tr><td>Plant Name</td><td>Date Planted</td></tr>
</table>

Water Requirements

Sunlight

☐ Seed   ☐ Transplant

Date	Event

Notes

Outcome

Uses

Purchased at: _______________________________   Price: _______________

Plant Name   **Date Planted**

Water
Requirements   🌢 🌢🌢 🌢🌢🌢   Sunlight ☼ ☼ ⬤

☐ Seed   ☐ Transplant

Date	Event

Notes

Outcome

Uses

Purchased at: _______________________________   Price: _______________

Plant Name	**Date Planted**

Water Requirements

Sunlight

☐ Seed   ☐ Transplant

Date	Event

Notes

Outcome

Uses

Purchased at: _______________________________ Price: __________

Plant Name	**Date Planted**

Water Requirements 💧 💧💧 💧💧💧

Sunlight

☐ Seed   ☐ Transplant

Date	Event

Notes

Outcome

Uses

Purchased at: _______________________________   Price: _______________

Plant Name

Date Planted

Water Requirements

Sunlight

Seed

Transplant

Date	Event

Notes

Outcome

Uses

Purchased at: ___________________________________

Price: ___________________

Plant Name   **Date Planted**

Water
Requirements   Sunlight

☐ Seed   ☐ Transplant

Date	Event

Notes

Outcome

Uses

Purchased at: ______________________________________   Price: ________________________

Plant Name   **Date Planted**

Water
Requirements   Sunlight

☐ Seed   ☐ Transplant

Date	Event

Notes

Outcome

Uses

Purchased at: ______________________________   Price: ______________

| **Plant Name** | **Date Planted** |

Water Requirements

Sunlight

☐ Seed   ☐ Transplant

Date	Event

Notes

Outcome

Uses

Purchased at: _________________________   Price: _________________________

Plant Name   **Date Planted**

Water Requirements 　　　　Sunlight

☐ Seed　　　☐ Transplant

Date	Event

Notes

Outcome

Uses

Purchased at: ______________________________________　　Price: ____________